N 12204

3 05.25 "

"W 4700

03.26"N

122043'

3 .19"e

'07.25"N 129059'15.09"W 44013'

"N 76028'39.74"W

"N

04'45.65"W 52052'

00.

D0746349

73"W 44010'12.57"N 77   50'

25'46.04"N 123024'05.76"W 5401

29"N 130017'13.13"W 48026'18.10

031'50.42"W 47002'53.87"N 8018'

'e 53055'06.72"N 122043'39.25"W

3'44.48"N 76028'39.74"W 44013'

"N 76028'39.74"W 48026'18.10"N

1'50.42"W 42021'40.67"N 71002'3

W 44013'44.48"N 76028'39.74"W

3'44.48"N 76028'39.74"W 48024'

"N 89011'13.64"W 43032'46.07"N

4'55.86"W 44031'35.21"N 122041'

W 45038'09.35"N 75055'35.85"W

0'38.52"N 79021'02.02"W 45024'

'N 75037'35.47"W 36047'40.84"N

40'53.56"W 33045'34.96"N 11801

Sarah de Leeuw

geographies of a lover

NeWest Press

copyright Sarah de Leeuw 2012

LIBRARY AND ARCHIVES CANADA CATALOGUING IN PUBLICATION

de Leeuw, Sarah
Geographies of a lover / Sarah de Leeuw.

Poems.
ISBN 978-1-897126-78-3

I. Title.

PS8607.E4827G46 2012   C811'.6   C2011-906750-1

Editor for the Board: Hiromi Goto
Cover photo: Briar Craig
Author photo: Briar Craig

NeWest Press acknowledges the financial support of the Alberta Multimedia Development Fund and the Edmonton Arts Council for our publishing program. We further acknowledge the financial support of the Government of Canada through the Canada Book Fund (CBF) for our publishing activities. We acknowledge the support of the Canada Council for the Arts which last year invested $24.3 million in writing and publishing throughout Canada.

#201, 8540–109 Street
Edmonton, Alberta T6G 1E6
780.432.9427
NeWest Press www.newestpress.com

No bison were harmed in the making of this book.

printed and bound in Canada by Gauvin Press   1 2 3 4 5 13 12

There is no angle the world can assume which the love in my eye cannot make into a symbol of love. Even the precise geometry of his hand, when I gaze at it, dissolves me into water...

ELIZABETH SMART
By Grand Central Station I Sat Down and Wept
1945

CONTENTS

DISTANCE

Something terrible may one day happen to you.

A car accident in the countryside when you are collecting
two new kittens for your children. A random act of terrorism
in a café you nipped into while looking for a book of poetry
(perhaps even for me). A subway derailment as you travel to
work after making breakfast for your family. A heart attack
on a Tuesday morning. A drunk driver careening into a busy
sidewalk. A misstep on the stairs of your university's fire exit.
Or, much more likely, something small and without reason
or warning.

I would never know.

Our lines of communications would just end.

Maybe you finally had second thoughts, or feelings of guilt,
and lacked the courage to tell me.

Maybe the time finally came when you chose your family
over me.

It would be my burden to respect not hearing from you. Those
who love you like I do, your wife, your children, your in-laws
and family members, they would be the ones to plan details.
In the ways that loved ones do. With phone lists and contact
sheets and word of mouth.

I am a detail impossible to factor in.

Distance is what defines a lover.

I am far from waking up beside you day after day. I am separate
from leaking windows and weeds in the driveway. I am beyond
a kitchen sink with dishes calling.

I will never experience mourning you publicly.

I will never see how your youngest child brought you close to tears
by asking why red finger paint looks so much like the blood of
that woman you all saw in a faraway place last night on TV

it's as though you are shoving yourself into me with no warning,
bone dry and unexpected, lights shatter inside my retina, blood
vessels rupturing, a searing that forces my wide eyes open, the
very opposite of canoeing the kasiks river in northern british
columbia, paddles gently edging through the water, wet and
giving when we found ourselves in a side channel with large
alder trees and cottonwoods and the reaching vine maples when
suddenly beside us, in a silver snag on the edge of thick green
water, three juvenile owls sitting grey brown mottled and blinking
high pitched whistling like a dream of the apocalypse i am in
this city alone anticipating the possibility of your arrival knowing
it is unlikely i glance toward the mountains on the other side of
the saint lawrence and decide to experience jean-paul riopelle
alone, his paintings make me feel like sobbing, standing before
his tribute to rosa luxemburg opens me up, standing alone, the
owls calling and riopelle's owls hurt they are such perfect images,
each of his works, he says, is a first time with the experience of
those that have come before it, the owls like knives oh why does
your absence have such a presence? my expectation more ripe
than if it were fulfilled the hills across the river from quebec city
only just touched with snow they too are waiting, the leaves still
in monumental colour riopelle's paintings thick and full like wind
canvases bursting open and out like you might do in my cunt
if you were here but in your stead i am left fractured by a putty
knife remembering the young owls, slow blinking heads swiveling
i pretend not to notice your absence try not to look behind me
hoping you might appear unexpectedly expectedly i think i hear
the owls calling each other, the loneliest of calls, ripping at me
from the inside out.

this tender wound is my missing your body, standing on a lake shore with the sun at my back, my shadow-outline fractured into filaments and halo shards broken into summer fattened fish i dissolve into thick overlapping scales, protective but useless against a hurt that is nothing at all, the nothing of emptiness gaping between rock edges torn apart from millennia of seismic shuddering, of sky wedges visible between red cedar roots upended and hurled into driftwood with tide stripped-back bark, the nothing of the unlit moon when it rises far from full and we simply trust that what is not visible exists, like you, not here with your hips settling against my lower back you not here with your thumb in my mouth you not here with your hand resting between my upper thighs and you are not a river during break-up full against banks straining through muscled ice blocks nor are you the wrist-thick sturdy roots of water lilies wedged firmly into muskeg bogs warm below the line of decomposition, you are certainly not and this aches.

42°59'03.26"N 81°13'05.25"W

we meet in the wet heat of summer when leaves appear like water
evaporating and trees are breathing yellow haze in a southern
ontario sky flower gardens entering their prime a mixture of lilac
and factories, a mist rising from lawns sloping into the night your
thigh stays persistently pressed to me so i do not move under the
table for over six hours imagine the concentration, etching lines
into a zinc plate would take less time the lines of your muscles
forcing themselves into my blood stream through my spine
into my nipples the base of my cunt feeling your leg you talk
with everyone around us we do not know each other but speak
animatedly the great lakes still cool having not yet acclimatized
to summer temperatures i think of asking you to reach down,
please slip a finger into me, but instead hold the thought inside
me looking at you closely, two complete strangers, i notice an
exhausted dip to your right eye a graying hair on your right ear
lobe the sparrows are beginning to make nests darting under eves
the starlings white-eyed and mean anticipating anything at all
possible chestnut trees have the broadest foliage of everything in
sight your leg against me begins my travel across the continent i
feel like masturbating to every mile of highway driving consistent
vibration the landscapes push into me clenching one hand on the
wheel i follow personal rhumb lines south west then north then
due west memory a combustible fuel i come through landscapes
through the dakota badlands through the national grasslands
through rusted rock outcroppings through fields full of blackened
sunflowers through marshes hovering in mist and moving with
pelicans through fresh snow on silvered sage lands through the
foothills of the rocky mountains through wide open montana
skies and i am coming to a thought of muscle and bone unknown

fully clothed the pressure of a stranger memory made material etched i do nothing but imagine you slipping into me i slip my fingers inside myself driving and coming our meeting immaterial and what i imagine becomes something to hold tight, the road droning under me the horizon outside the car bending an open endless movement.

warm lack of darkness is your absence, i miss your forget-me-not
blue cock veins like vines on a rough limestone surface, if you
were here i would say ease into me illuminated in the half light,
bending as malleably as the hooves on a newly born moose calf,
softened bone they slip unharming against the great walls of
vaginal track, kicking and struggling to stand upright i would
do the opposite, laying back anywhere for you, especially here
on the sharp brittle bite of forest floor, needles of conifers, pine
trees perishing by the millions in northern british columbia a
landscape as raw red and dying as the lands of my reddened cunt,
an epidemic of loss, muscles like exhausted ravens grieving their
fist-sized chicks, bundles of feathered blackness fallen from nests
and splayed flightless at the base of trees from upon which they
call with voices cracked as my abdomen, cramping in emptiness,
that unsatisfactory forging with my own hands does nothing
but accentuate the long reach of rivers remembered, a repeated
meandering of riffle, pool, riffle, pool and at some point i have
simply ceased to battle the current.

P L A C E

Before you knocked on the door of room 1091, wearing a wonderful grey felt hat and a shirt the colour of a cloudless summer sky, the room felt uninhabited.

The door nothing but a thin wood veneered object with a fake brass handle opening onto four nondescript walls. Two single beds, a yellowed plastic lamp stand, a telephone beige with age, a desk topped with a television, a coffee maker, and two cellophane wrapped glasses.

Then you arrived in room 1091.

Nothing changed, but nothing remained the same.

As you passed them, every meaningless article transformed into something worth remembering. The loose-legged chair. You sat in front of the window and I touched your damp forehead and kissed your hair. The gold synthetic duvet covers. We pushed the beds together and spread them over a re-sized mattress and you pulled off my t-shirt and we saw each other naked for the first time. The curtains, slightly water stained. You closed them because it is mid-morning when you arrive and the city is awake and we do not want people to see us making love, which we have never done before. The two thin pillows. You stack them and rest your head on them the second time we make love, this time very silently with you beneath me, eyes closed.

How to describe the transformation of things from meaningless to memorable? Of nameless to intimately known?

The difference is tangible but invisible.

Just like we all know the sun's warmth on an August afternoon feels nothing at all like the sun's warmth at midday in January.

the headwaters of this orgasm, this blue, begin somewhere in
switzerland, a drowning in paul klee's tableau de poissons, a
shaking of blue hues sparkling fish floating at sea, your weight
full length on top of me, your cock slowing, a start, a prelude to
quick thrusts, the flashes of light, a current, shelves of turquoise
ice sun-slivered shards stacked in the skeena river's throat, cliffs
of icicles dripping and the taste of my own cunt as you slide into
my mouth and back again and when did i start swallowing your
cum with you up so close your pulse, the vein in your leg at the
base of your hip against my chin, little dipper birds dipping in the
strips of water that ice hasn't yet swallowed up, their wings in the
clear flow, swimming birds surrounded by wind racing over snow
smoothing a high gloss shine like the skin of your cock, tight,
and i am fucking tight around you, you tell me this, as my sides
loosen, the huffing of a moose running across a clearcut, scent
of wolf not so far away, clouds of breath, nostrils splayed, a valley
that bends before a running animal, the streams of warm air
from sub-alpine, the memory of klee in a city but my body an
estuary-place, mouth opening on the pacific ocean where you
have poured into me, the way you cup my jaw and jack yourself
off into my mouth, the way you say i am going to come, shit oh
shit and then the deluge that breaks blue inside me, spots of blue,
a wall of blue, wet and unstopped salty you remember to thank
me, fingers still inside.

alaskan panhandle tipped in turquoise glacier veins slide through
valleys the late night early morning moment when you wet two
fingers with spit and slip them inside me even though i'm asleep
the following afternoon our feet are slipping on shale and black
lichen like lace on moraine skree walls of graveled ice mammoth
before us you don't wait for me to awaken fully placing your hands
on my hips lifting me my face still down where glaciers melt into
mud-silver lakes ice caves gape open dripping dangerous they
growl from miles within their melting sounds painful with great
cliffs of sky blue ice crashing down you enter me with a fast one
stroke forcing my chin against ribs arms bent elbows braced in the
distance the far edge of the brandon glacier an abandoned mine
rusts armature exposed as concrete decomposes surrounded by
ruins of iron and cable slowly overtaken with tiny purple flowers,
alpine fireweed, and in the meadows beyond the ice fields aster
and paintbrush listen to glaciers calving exhaling rivers rushing
over upturned root systems, fingers threading through water you
pull out of me, everything but the very tip of your cock exposed
and then back inside in this position you can reach around me
fully encircle me to rub my clit thrusting we are silent as your
balls slap me, outside thin streams trickle off glaciers' sides the
slide alder and altitude wizened engelmann spruce so green the
needles almost black the surface of the glacier pitted with smooth
blue lips snow lined or the velvety silt several feet thick on the
bottom of small pools in alpine i've fixed my wrist in my mouth
to maintain a quiet concentration as you fuck me from behind
the speed of glacier retreats escalating with climate change a
rapid withdrawal up valleys toward the comparative coolness of
mountain tops soon there may be nothing left of the ice bodies

and it feels as though a knotted leash of pumping blood connects
my cunt to the pulse in my neck skin thudding like the heart of
reptile in your hand i'm swimming inside my skin my body an
umbilical cord of cirques and glacial till you collapse against my
back face buried in my shoulder blades we are breathing like
crevasses meeting summer.

bulrushes and pampas grasses broken down by winter wind and
the everywhere freeze and thaw, the lakeshore cracking waves
frozen in whipped peaks ice buckling spanning back where
black edges of open water lap against a thin white perimeter
encircling gravel and stones, cracked frost-like dried cum on the
line of my jawbone you fucked my mouth like the lake in winter
it takes forever, before you blow open exhausted the ice expands
enveloping water marks left in ochre fields where puddles have
evaporated, shadow imprints remain, circles of dried salt indented
in earth my mouth dry, muscles aching saliva thick and sparse
eyes closed the feel of semen drying, a crackling trace in my right
dimple, the sound of ice collecting and rattling like stalks of grass
bending as cars pass by.

52°12'16.512"N   129°04'45.65"W

you're not thinking of the bears outside, your tongue working
inside of me, great brown bodies with muscles knotted at
their shoulders, fishing in the stink of mating bodies flesh
green purple guts working at the gravel eggs and sperm under
salmon spawning a last clutch of bodies before they become
carcasses ceasing to fight the current, the smell of grey wool
blankets bunched and scratching under my shoulders it doesn't
matter, my sweat attracting mosquitoes in the heat of august
red sockeye with their mallard green heads filling the streams
as if to overflow the banks my cunt has never been so wet,
you've been working for ages, the lava beds forget there is such
a thing as night in these long northern summer days when the
sky is always lit, a perfect fire season this year, the fish running
strong, the grizzlies fat and glossy, the other loggers listening
at the door of the room at the end of the bunkhouse the only
room with a woman now shaking wet twisting head back
calling out your name, the men have seen you at the dump
with me when we are watching grizzlies eat from bags full of
everything people have no use for, somehow you're working
me simultaneously with your tongue and two fingers, but we
are fascinated with how delicate those massive animals can be,
claws pulling apart black plastic careful to choose disposable
TV dinner containers and cans still slick with remnants of food,
the bears lick each container gently great clawed paws cradling
forgotten confectionary, pork and beans or pudding or salisbury
steak, although the salmon are thick enough to scoop like olives
from the brine the bears still crave human garbage, perhaps a
taste they experience nowhere else, a taste they come to crave,
like my voice that has given out my throat dry and useless all i

can do is hold your head in my hands hold you down your scalp
full of grit from a day in the bush logging sawdust spit out in an
arch toward your face the sounds of great trees falling hemlock
and spruce and red cedar a clean smell mixed with fungus lichen
and mushrooms wind carried off the lava beds rock hot baking in
the sun, dry leaves like kindling charring, igniting slipping into
invisible passages deep in lava flows then catching, lighting, root
systems on the flow's edge, the grizzlies lift their faces to the wind
smelling the world burning they rise with their arms outstretched
shaking their fur rolling in waves of wetness when the fish are this
abundant the bears eat selectively choosing nothing but brain,
cool and fat-heavy to build winter bulk i've finished i can't come
again i'm am exhausted unable to fight the current, listening to
the hollow snorting grunting of grizzlies pacing outside these
thin wood paneled bunkhouse walls.

TOPOGRAPHY

Late at night under bright lights, you oversee men laying the oil pipeline. The pipe is smaller, more fragile, than you had once imagined. Less than six feet in diameter, the walls only a few inches thick. Flexible galvanized steel, memory-metal designed to move, to bend across the ups and downs between countries and borders.

No one but you will agree to supervise the pipeline construction, these rough-neck men. So you go. After you leave, I stew rhubarb and contemplate the heights of mountains in Alaska and the piles of displaced earth in Alberta's tar sands.

The men under your watch sweat and shine as they work, opening a dirty wound alongside the highway where fireweed will go to seed in the fall, leaves suddenly bright orange.

You call me late at night, hands aching from holding the thick chains that maneuver sections of pipe into the earth. You tell me the billboard outside your hotel reads: "Best Rooms in Town, Only Bar."

In some sections the cuts are so steep that it is impossible to fully stem the steady stream of rubble tumbling into the trench. The men complain of boulders and danger.

When you and I are alone, you lay me flat on your bed and cover me fully with the weight of your body. You assure me I am safe under your watch.

Once after making love I dreamt I was driving along the highway, parallel to the pipeline, searching for your worksite.

Cliffs came down vertically on both sides and ahead I saw a transport truck rushing toward me.

For a moment the rig appeared to levitate, hovering above the ground, wheels in a bottomless fog.

ponderosa pines popping like thin-walled bubbles, igniting
against sulfur ridge, elk running hooves held high eyes rolling
with panic, the whites reflecting all of british columbia burning
and across maligne lake we watch a fire start, first a thin finger of
flame then grey smoke billowing the air shaking with helicopters,
evacuation notices, and fire events can be charted through
charcoal records, lake cores and sediment carefully separated,
frequency and magnitude of burns calculated i wonder if my cunt
would produce such records long dry spells we can't explain, once
almost a month, and even in our tent where usually we fuck so
well i'm convinced your nails are jagged your mouth scratches the
road sides are on fire at night the ground crisscrossed with wounds
spewing orange molten ground slipping into small ponds, birds
with nowhere to land the horizon grey-yellow we make clumsy
efforts to fuck your cock leaking across my stomach you can't
convince me and i let you slide into me without conviction the
smell of smoke in our hair in our clothes and you make effort to
undress me slowly, considerately, but there's something crawling
under my skin unquenchable a raven flying too low caught on
the wing by a spark feathers burning images of families watching
homes disappear sage brush fire starter lichen and moss evaporate
in the heat entire mountain sides with bed rock exposed tree
trunks nothing but ruined black sticks: by looking at the walls of
my womb, could you tell what spoilage was left? carbon dating
tells only part of the story, tree coring another small puzzle solved
the rings an autobiography of fires over time but the lines of
charcoal are steady and true all the way from mcbride through to
the rocky mountains and down again into the prairies your cock
is hard for weeks bumping into me, you try putting mouth on my

neck and i know your need to fuck me hurts like a forest fire, it's the intervals scientists have a difficult time explaining, wanting to predict for the future if only to prevent the disaster of that summer landscapes brittle and dry the smallest of sparks unstoppable flames jumping rivers the sun shaking hot like a sore re-opened in the sky no rain for days and days and days i am preoccupied with images of blackened blistered fields leading to exposed foundations of homes at night the fires sound like an endless snapping of small twigs pebbles shaken in a tin can, but i can't concentrate, even with your cock in my mouth i'm thinking of animals inhaling smoke, lungs scorched and bursting, everything burning.

my cunt humming, moving by itself, the factories outside huge
power and hydro lines marshlands look ill between concrete and
grey and the cat tails exploding in the newly cool fall air reminding
me of you in my mouth, in my hand, coming as i pull you off,
pulling you out of sleep breaking open in my hand the gravel
outside the window on the edge of train tracks is loose and oily
with bits of wood ripped apart, tracks boxcars and livestock, the
feel of cock between solid and soft, finished you lick your thumb,
make the edge of your hand slick to run it against the length
of my cunt lips pumping your thick thumb inside me i become
useless for anything but lying on my back pushing my gut cunt
hips upward, wanting pressure to never let up, wanting everything
to stop blurring, wanting nothing to focus the red and yellow and
orange leaves outside are so beautiful, the sky blue to my right fields
of corn past those the lake the imposing lines of cranes moving
soil, breaking earth, another expanse of hydro lines, then white
contrails of airplanes like tracks, lines of canada geese flying low,
a cement factory grey particle dust almost hurtful to the small
winding stream we pass two men standing in the late morning air
fishing and surrounded by everything changing the landscape of
marshes and lakeside, i wonder too if my body will change over
time, lifting itself hard, almost humiliating myself, as if it is nothing
but what it demands, as i tighten and flex inside myself doing this
surrounded by strangers, ropy thick streams brown glistening under
the train tracks and the bed is soft and caving inward beneath me
as i ask for the full thickness of your weight upon me, bear down,
rest full on my ribs and lungs, pushed inward and catching the
sumac the brightest of all like a hot coal at the edge of the fire pit,
thick base to tapered tip reaching the clouds touching the lake,

pewter outlined in white, backlit by sun late morning light on cut
down corn stalks aligned and glinting, how painful to walk across
such a field barefoot two crows calling against another factory
then the shore line becomes trees and green marsh waters with
lily pads i fill my own fist with saliva open palmed like a water
lily leaf flatten wetness on my cunt so you can slip back and forth
against me, behind me, from behind, behind me now in the
train two women speaking about the national ballet of canada,
one of them a choreographer, i imagine bodies bending under
pressure, unbreakable but aching, muscles taut and the train stops
momentarily to let more people in and now we are moving, another
train rushing past on the left, breathless, a thick roar crashing like
the sound of the ocean, inhaling and exhaling, metal waves on
tracks i'm on top of you so my ass opens up as you slip out of me,
the power lines running parallel to the train tracks form a hairline
split, a crack, across the horizon an unending black thread, white
gulls lifting up in one choreographed group from the newly tilled
black soil, you sit up after insisting i fuck your fingers harder you
wonder for a moment about the sappy wetness just above your knee
and it takes a moment, just a moment, to realize i've come so hard
it's a watershed yellow flowers holding on precarious amongst the
dying ocher grasses we're moving so slowly the open mouths of
milkweed pods are entirely visible, smooth and gold inside, such a
fine cradle for the seeds expelled to the wind, it's only the odd bit
of white that remains, hanging alone in the home that cultivates
it, piles of creosoted ties stacked on the tracks that grass has taken
over, an autumn field and in its centre stands an oak tree bent and
buckled, torn but not broken and in the following field stand two
horses when i woke you up last night urgent for your cock in my

mouth the shrubs outside change from red to purple as i once
again feel your heavy slowness roll on top of me, my knees up
my legs touching your shoulder blades ankles touching your waist
and then dressing and then moving down in the elevator together
a final slow falling on the way to your car, to the train, to these
landscapes hurtling by.

you used your teeth and hands to grasp the edge of the atlantic
coastline, your hands still wounded and scarred, a transformation
into articulated digits from fins your new lungs gasping great gulps
of breath free at last from the grey metal haul of that military frigate
you'd served on for five years, the waves crashing cold in the late
winter evening, sand meeting shrubbery's intricate black arterioles,
sap resting in root systems the atlantic still wedged somewhere in
your abdomen i feel my own stomach tighten when i so much as
turn and catch a movement of your hands, they could not have
been intended for anything but sex, sex and hauling yourself up
onto the land, a sea creature transformed to land dweller you insist
you will never again set foot on the surface of any body of water
but your journey across my body is oceans, at first you shared the
coast with herring and gulls and cormorants, the rocky nova scotia
shoreline much more formidable than its pacific counterpart,
halifax is your first port stop tentative steps on the boardwalk, so
close to ocean, slick with frost it would be so easy to fall back into
the chuck, and there are so many navy boats, they call out your
name drowned only by the barking of seals the slippery twisting
roads from city to open ocean you learn of halifax's great fire and
it stirs in you a great fear of evaporation, a greater need to leave,
in an airplane because of the speed and the lack of water involved,
you flee to the pacific coast red cedar and more herring, once when
we are making love i become certain there is phosphorescence
covering my hands and you explain how herring glow moments
after they've died, blue silver green smooth scales tiny perfect fins
alight with phosphorescence and when you worked for the military
standing on the deck of that killing ship surrounded by nothing
but sky and sea black under clouds you imagined the landscapes

below the surface, kelp beds and rock cod, everything silent, mountains swaying to tides puffins like bullets with orange and white faces tracking silver darts, you had gills once again, diving down, like mercury breaking, specks, the silver smoothness of a herring school every element moving together chasing light lifting your hands open me, breathing ocean and breaking horizons, phosphorescence spilling you've grasped the raw of edge of my climax holding on with teeth and hands you haul yourself out and up onto dry land.

S C A L E

The moments between us are so tiny.

If we thought love was monumental, we were right.

It is monumentally small, beyond comprehension, an impossible thing to grasp.

You see, I love you with the same force as the smallest and most tragic instant I know. The instant when a pillow fell to the floor, to the left of the bed, resting in a streak of sunlight, on a curl of overlooked dust and pubic hair. The instant she was napping, thin lines of saliva, shallow inhalations, the instant when her baby died. The most tragic instant I know.

She may never forgive herself for not waking up during those sliver-seconds of death, for not witnessing the precise moment when her baby stopped breathing, motionless in a twist of sheets, still against the curve of her upper arm.

This is the desperate scale at which I love you.

making love in the morning, oolichan running close to the
river's surface, days of early spring and the nights still long,
a perpetual greyness in the northwest coast sky small silver
fish twisting in the beaks of gulls converging by the thousands
on the skeena river on the nass river, after a thousand times or
more inside of me the rhythm is perfectly matched and at low
tide the mud flats smell slightly of salt the ocean reaching this
far inland eel grass wet bent, seals gorging, round bodies with
eagles overhead slow flying barely a flicker of movement in
their outstretched wings then a quick collapse and closing tight
like a fist hammering their bodies drop i like to hoist my cunt
upward and watch you lean back both hands on my hip bones
wrenching my body harder i can reach down and feel you, in
out in, with my finger the ice still not broken up on sections of
the rivers, monstrous blocks of graveled snow blue and black
with salt speckles and once at high tide, the ice flows rushing
groaning as they pour downriver, at the mouth of the skeena,
we witness an eagle dig her talons into the back of a salmon too
large to lift from the water, that muscled hunting bird banging
wings on water awkward swimming salmon wrenching the
eagle must have been so exhausted when the fish was finally
pulled ashore, she ripped into the guts and faced sideways a
fast pumping of blood and sometimes if you stand very still
on the edge of the skeena you can hear avalanches, snow pack
loosening and rushing, like water down mountain sides or
granite faces, years later the slices through tree line scar over
with slide alder and salmon berry bushes and as you pull out
of me there's a sound like dogs running across seaweed on mud,
the wet ground trying desperately to coax paws back down,

a resistance to release, in the estuary everything is waiting, balanced between fresh water and ocean, bodies acclimatizing, there is that tiny space of time in the morning just between night and day when my body is thickly full and once again tired although i've only just awoken.

48026'18.10"N 68031'50.42"W

holler out my name, loud as a jet stream interrupting v's of
geese calling forth the north in uninterrupted blue sky with
sounds that echo like shouting in the steep canyons of ridgeback
mountains, treelines low and bare rock exposing itself open to
clouds and the cirque of my stomach above pubic hairline where
a glinting edge of pre-cum is caught, it is sunlight fractured
by a crow's wing, brightness that makes you blink as if briefly
pierced by a devil's club thorn, prehistoric leaves so large they
are horizons unto themselves and above them grow furled
fisted bulbs ripening in the scent of cottonwood sap, spring,
spring is yelling and hardening again inside me even though
you just finished roots are shaking themselves awake ready to
break soil anew you exhale like a moan calling the onset of an
early morning storm, unexpected, mouth around my nipple the
blossoms of maple trees fattening in my cunt you are urging
me to move over you again because when winter retreats the air
is noisy with everything that snow and frost made silent so we
are calling out to each other, yelling the possibility of muscles
aching from fucking like the season depends on us, we are
bringing in summer, coming.

snow on vineyards core of this winter city split by a river slipped
through with swans swimming, necks arched hissing stretched
outside our hotel room window and you whispering, hoarse and
caught in the back of your throat, treat my cock viciously, stop
being gentle, i push aside fears i might hurt you and i fuck you
so hard with my hand that i ache with the wet sound of wings
beating, breaking surface tension, great feathered bodies lifting,
lilting over centuries-old wooden covered bridges, water on the
brink of freezing, thick hardening slices of snow converging i
grip harder than i ever imagined i could, slamming my fist up
and down i want the mottled white cum, coloured like urban
swans, slippery in my palm or, if you tell me just before you are
ready, in my mouth, i am concentrating on nothing else, not the
city sounds of heels on cobblestones or the smell of chocolates
and cigarettes or the snow starting to fall again, i am on my
knees my cunt wet, wrist sore, that glove of skin over bone-hard
blood moving under my grip i love the moment when you say
i am going to come, i am going to come, and engines ignite
in the narrow alleys outside and someone coughs far away and
the sky is fattened full with snow still to fall and i have never
swallowed faster.

no one is needed, the horizon a sunset against red osier dogwood
or cranberry bogs or the rushing sap of vine maples, bleeding
times and i am digging in, deep, under the skin slick as deer fat
the freshness of meat hanging ripe guts left in coils on rainforest
moss and lichens bristly short-haired and tender with everything
i bring myself to rusted waters coloured from tannin i lie back with
the gorged body of a tick full from burrowing, we know ourselves
better than anyone, a slip down around and into shedding, the
deep brown of arbutus bark sloughing slowly as the trunk expands,
rhythmic and alone.

face pale, snow in the air but not yet falling, seagulls on ice on
a still evening lake against shores of broken grey slate your eyes
sharp as mica embedded in the rare bruised rock of nights passing
without sleep, barely time to catch our breath the pulse of small
fish winding together inside waves, backlit bodies catching light
shadows on the ocean floor just inside me is oyster-like translucent
sky my exhausted skin damaged as the body of a spawning salmon,
the cream of herring's sperm on roe on kelp, eggs by the millions,
the colour of trapped or settled smoke, we need to sleep, we need
to sleep, but already you are turning toward me.

44°13'44.48"N   76°28'39.74"W

november sky storm orange wind filthy tearing with lightning
strikes, tree leaves still yellow the rain pounding against pavement,
torn clouds shredded grey and rupturing, one side of the horizon
almost black pewter, then rainbows slivering into the thunder
claps, the lake hurling itself against limestone, slabs like scales
of prehistoric creatures wet with waves the other side of the sky
recovering blue i am laying on my back watching the weather,
cum and bits of broken condom seeping out of me, my cunt a
squall and all i can dream of is richard brautigan's springhill mine
disaster taking place in my womb, i want the storm to rip right
through me leaving nothing in its wake.

MAPPING

Four feet of snow have fallen overnight, the temperature dipping
below minus 34 and falling.

A new terrain is born, uncharted lands between my front door
and the sidewalk's edge. Old markers have vanished. I am
directionless as I shovel, reduced to guessing where lawn meets
driveway, where road meets property line.

Forty-nine days have passed since we made love and then you
returned home.

You have since sent me photos of your holidays. I stare at your
four-year-old daughter. She painted her fingernails gold. Her
grandfather looks like you. In one image, on a bookcase to his
left, is a photo of you with your wife, both younger.

I clear a path, shoveling to uncover details stored in memory.
The scar beneath your bottom lip. The darkened trail of hair
down your abdomen, wet from lying in my bathtub. The tips
of your cuspid teeth. The dips of skin between your fingers.

Atlases were once my favorite books. Legends comprised of
symbols that made perfect sense and little dots of all the places
I would travel.

The rarity of rhumb lines, stoic in their precision. If I lost
confidence I could follow their constancy to the ends of this
earth.

bodies balanced fragile as the weight of a bird, hollow bones
and avian frame barely bending the top branch of an aspen tree
upon landing but still in that split second of tucking in wings
the horizon shifts, is rearranged above new snow, fitted closely
over grey ground and i am reaching, bending too, tucking in and
asking that you move down, harder, now harder again, an osprey's
line of sight tilts at the edges, upwards like a wingspan on the
briefest flicker of warm air i'm pulling up so my face is close to
yours, breath the smell of frost when the noise of wind changes
from old fall leaves rattling to spring, when they are bursting
with green so green it is yellow, small birds disappear in foliage,
nothing but their voices visible, we emit calls at these moments,
calls for more, don't stop, because the rain will arrive and when
it falls quickly the ground is churned to froth, i am almost there,
a loosened sense of gut and eyelid, tendon stretching beneath hip,
that moment when a shadow passes over a field of snow geese and
in unison they rise, startled into flight, the smallest tips of black
counterbalancing white bodies, necks long thin and stretched
towards the not quite attainable direction of somewhere south.

tracks shaking under us red line silver line we read the poster 'rub
against me and i will expose you' part of this city's crackdown on
subway harassment we laugh against each other, stand too close,
rub me because i want you breast on elbow one hand on the steel
pole the other touching my neck your breath on my lips we do
nothing at all but talk of fucking your hips are pressed into the
subway seats alighting from the underground into sunlight and
decayed landscapes now gentrifying we walk close our only chance
to touch i picture your cock hard inside your jeans and think about
how you could hold me against the gallery wall as birds fly across
the floor an exhibit projected from above any chance we have in
this two-day window of time we try to connect the greatest possible
surface area of our bodies, a never-ending challenge, on street
benches on docks on sea-wall rocks on buses and trains and on the
sharp edges of sidewalks i tell you everything will be fine your wife
and children safe because we will stop before that moment of hard
cock a place of no turning back, boundary between open mouthed
kiss, soft heartbeat hammering and i want to feel the inside of your
lips then the tip of your cock the scrubbiness of chest hair against
my tits subway tracks gritty and screeching i think i would ask
you to finger fuck my ass, that unacceptable out-of-place request
i should not ask but this city allows it, thin streets with blurry vistas
we eat octopus and talk about swallowing cum, chat aimlessly about
fisting and public sex and geography and cities around the world
and we finish with lemon gelato, leave levitating feet off the ground
in this city of marathons, our bodies tightened and knotted and
worn down to the nub of resisting and resisting there is still a place
on my clavicle where you touched me the longest but abstinence
in this fucking city is fulfilling, a warm and perfect place.

sitting beside me but i want you inside of me outside the sky is
noisy with one thousand red-winged blackbirds and a thousand
more in flight through the leafless gold filaments of weeping
willow branches defoliated i look at your fingers, perfect thin bent
and resting together i hope you are thinking they could be in me,
not on your knees we listen to a harpsichordist flying through the
brandenburg concertos playing glass-like notes the way rhizomes
swell outward through the soil, brilliant breakable at the tips, my
nipples so hard they are tight as plucked strings or hail falling on
glass reflecting silver undersides of spruce needles, sharp pointed
ends and ridged when rolled between fingers or the sap left behind
after touching fir bark you could pull out of me, an almost humid
resistance from an inside that i would ensure had no ending the
blinding orange of blackbird's wings concentrated blood in my clit
all the flat marshlands that thaw slowly after winter, rushes and
reeds reaching up from smooth water still as granite, we would
disturb flat smoothness as fast as the flute enters bach's music and
you could bend toward me, listening closely for a lapsed note, the
violinist has no idea how her bow is sawing at the knot lodged into
my pelvis, my breath fast as light refracting through stained glass
and you remain uncomfortably not inside me.

you have a bird's eye view, the city stretched and slippery at your
feet, an ice storm encasing streets roofs chimneys billboards
and signs in neon, no, no we say, male pigeons full throat
plumage puffed with possibility, colours of gasoline on water
smooth grey etched by bright green and purple shifting feathers
unsettle like your arms beside mine the rain noisy against the
bedroom window, our breaths held, in parking lots in the endless
pavement sea i feel agitated, our decision to abstain scratching
the ground, a small fevered animal, any moment now branches
might snap from the sidewalk, trees made heavy with the freeze
with sleet and people have ceased to make their ways home,
the city shimmers dangerous and impassable and your leg
makes it over mine but stops there, a pedestrian caught on the
smallest of inclines, glass smooth surface, traffic oncoming,
such treacherous moments although by morning everything will
be salted, sheets of ice pitted and pockmarked, water dripping
from trees and leaving small scars on snow, the echo of birds'
feet still form circled paths on the frost.

CONTOUR LINES

She carves moments for herself. Away from family. Away from
you and the children. In these scarce times, your wife harvests
rainbow chard and armfuls of kale from raised garden beds.
By stacking old tires one on top of the other, by encircling
roots with new layers of soil, each level another enticement for
renewed growth, she grows potatoes that you wash, roast, and
turn into soups.

She spends spring and summer Saturdays on her knees, making
earth vertical. Produces slopes I will never achieve. Summits
with edges so steep their apexes make me dizzy with vertigo.

When you visit my house, it is a foreign altitude. The air is thin
with our nervousness. I offer you entirely different lines.

Hikes up an expired volcano, barren and sheer cliffs, lichen
encrusted, 180 degrees of wide open horizon.

The curved spans of moose carcasses, still warm, strapped down
under tarps in the back of pickup trucks.

The moving mounds of anthills making noise when we lean
very close.

I offer you my unmade bed and the crumpled edges of sheets
we can make love on at any time.

Lines so inconsequential and thin that balancing them may
become impossible.

48°24'33.20"N   89°11'13.64"W

i have never seen anything like this, an unending ocean of
freshwater bright green and not a single bite of salt, we begin
our descent traveling south though the province's north, north
country everywhere a group of seven painting white pines on
granite outcroppings or great stones breaking into lakes and
marsh lands where you shove my breasts together so harshly
they ache for days both my nipples fitting into your mouth, the
canadian shield is no harder, the soil thin and almost useless
all flora barely fixed but the red-winged black birds are moving
quickly across marshlands and flatness my nipples high and hard
are jutting between your teeth, you need not do anything more
than this, the car still running on the side of the road, i focus
on a quartz vein in relief hardened and protruding through
the smooth shield face and imagine touching the brittle stress
deformation cracks, the fault lines and dilation joints i know my
breasts will be chapped and split tomorrow, even the softest bra
will irritate, but i am surrounded by carmichael and macdonald
these two enfold me here the distant small islands balanced
in an endless lake, a lone pine foregrounded, an unending sky
stretched almost as though it hurts over choppy rocks and water
rushing headlong into the shield and i need to reach down for
myself, uncomfortable as you insist on biting deep, hard rock
scar and endless lake meeting island specks meeting sky, an ache
where the fissures have opened and hardened in your mouth,
in your mouth, in this land ridged and rigid like an oil painting.

43°32'46.07"N 80°14'55.86"W

please open your mouth wide like the horizon after sunset
reflects a city glowing distant pale blue-red haze on grey clouds
interrupted with lines of oak trees dense and interlocking like
my want to fill you with my tongue and teeth and fingers so
open your mouth against my cunt where lips meet teeth, a river's
drop-off, water careening over falls and the edges of boulders just
visible through churning froth, i look down, see your shoulders,
and i am holding in my hands your face a stretch of sky against
pastures in the winter corn stalks stock-still without wind the field
is motionless tension full before a drop in air pressure, sudden
snow open your mouth while you sink your thumb between my
teeth against my gums smooth as hailstones a signal of spring and
buds so bright and taut they look painful to touch your tongue
replaces your thumb and if i could take every part of you inside
me there would be room, a lake that seasonally disappears into
porous bedrock you coil around my back still fingering the roof of
my mouth and outside, a snow storm, because it's like i've busted
through gravel piled on top of me, lost all composure, a smolt
exposed to air, gills heaving, mouth open and craving the stream.

waking wet for weeks an agitated gut knotting and stomach tightening like some colony of humming insects nested right between my hip bones it hurts to walk to lie down my head back, redwood forests above me, sky laced the oregon coast the red cedars the sequoias so close to the ocean with rocks jutting from sand into mist but fucking is almost impossible sharing a tent trailer playing gin rummy or cribbage during the day my mind fixated on *the story of o*, belted down a small speck as men lined up to fuck every angle of her, even in our campsite the trees are massive thick root systems making it hard to back the trailer in and because it's an open space your brother is just inches away and we are loath to unwrap condoms so i press my back against you my asshole loose enough that you work yourself in, we lie almost still for easily an hour i can feel the pressure on my bowels can hear the waves and gulls muffled by redwoods thickness bark folds deep and irregular wide enough to slip an entire fist into my pelvis hard a sequoias' base, a tree does not flinch, unmoving and unmoved it considers transforms water and things far more worthy of consideration than *o* who is cut open imagine a tree cut into, felled i imagine them when you are inside me giant trees threading themselves together underground then reaching, reaching, skyward, limbs outstretched, the canopy green shadowing ground from sky.

BORDERLANDS

It is a searing migration, this walk over tarmac gap, this movement
from lounge to fuselage, this somewhere between being in your
arms and being back home, in separate countries.

A sparkling airport desert under cold bright sky. A dry liminal
land devoid of habitation. Asphalt, yellow lines, and wings.
We obey signs. We do not run backwards. We do not behave
suspiciously as our hearts shatter.

Lines between nations have always separated people from the
ones they love. Without regard to sinew or tendons stretched
to their limits. Without notice of aching. Of abandonment.
Of weeping in these swaths of guarded territory.

45°38'09.35"N   75°55'35.85"W

borderlands between ontario and quebec the ottawa river separates
topographic shifts from westerly flatness to the east hilled relief as
you slip up and beneath my shirt fingers pressuring trees bowed
and curved in semi-circles against rounded gradient you cup the
in-between space and ribcage lines are shallow valleys of snow
accumulation extended like worn skin stretch marked with layers
draped over the granite incursions that are flesh brown and shot
with purple-pink veins, your cock pushed between my breasts you
fuck new gradient, steep contours, and the hills with de-foliaged
tamaracks and white pines yellow cedars sumac berries puckered
are rigid nipples pinched as the landscapes bunch into small
mountains, the first in such a long time, lakes at every base and
rocky islands standing firm against incursion or erosion or the thick
seepages of water from thin crevasses the icicles suspended and
always about to break, below their pointed bases accumulate piles
of shattered shards, reminders of wetness under pressure, of falling,
of your knees digging into my sides and your stomach seizing and
near to my mouth you shove yourself between uprises, topography
rife with relief and release.

43°40'38.52"N 79°21'02.02"W

metal tip splitting sky and air, below us water sheds copper veins
reflecting the sun stretched against wingtips a thud of wheels
inhaled echoing through my gut muscles reverberating you seat
yourself beside me red osier dogwood thick with sap and visible as
rust, here, even from above, no touching no contact just speaking
and voice and the clouds sliced open against a lack of atmosphere
you ask me to imagine fucking two men, fingering a picture of
your wife and three children and the tamarack trees somewhere
beneath us are shedding needles, nothing but blackened etchings
from such a height your prick an air disturbance a jolt leaning
over and mouthing the word 'tit,' we are landing, landing, you
asking me to jerk you off as we descend into vancouver thick
warm mist replaces the toronto evening far away in frozen.

vision slips and in the distance a form lifts, an airplane solid as
your weight across my stomach the shape shifts still aggregate
a cliff a shear drop-off of earth into a west coast peninsula with
gulls coasting and desperate trees clinging to rock faces i turn my
face and the shape undoes along the edges, fragments detaching,
the airplane is coming apart, from the outside in, the great flying
mass breaking and you are rising again hardening against me
my gut fluttering i realize the form, solid in the sky silver on blue,
is nothing near metal but instead a flock of small birds converged
in a wind of insects, feeding as one but now, finished, they dart
apart while you push in again and i too come apart, everything
once solid a blink of birds tossed, small stones in the clouds.

36°47'40.84"N   108°40'53.56"W

a doubling then redoubling, monarchs touch down rest folded
and halved rusty bodies on purple clovers startled open becoming
twice themselves, wings, your two hands spreading on my shoulders
where bones meet sloping skin the temperature of high noon a
day of painted desert with shiprock rising in thick yellow heat
shuddering as if alive, doubling with shadow and mirage in the
dry air, then the sweat we contain slips loose with concentration,
condensation on my clavicle, sand cut open by flash floods, the
ground gashed with dry creek beds littered with small twigs, thorns
and leaves leaving a path down my spine your nails do not hurt
although they should inside me mesas doubling across monument
valley the body of a hawk hurling itself towards some invisible insect
that in an instant will break open in a beak, the pain a moment
before there is nothing but the sharp edge of desolation rocks and
range lands and you are fingering me wet where the splitting in
two is borderlands and migrating butterflies.

N O R T H

High Arctic whiteouts are not made of new, falling snow.
They are not caused by precipitation.

The fields of the circumpolar north are a desert. Rocks. Frozen
saltwater. Ice.

The wind loosens icy surfaces, whips up what is gnawed off,
recirculating it as if the sky were releasing moisture. What
blinds even dogs, what makes travel impossible, is a frenzy
of crystals carved from thousand-year-old glaciers.

Late at night, lost, I orient to an imagined you.

Impossibility is lost.

Your wife and children are no longer a magnetized pull home.

I am no longer an expedition.

You are with me, dipping teaspoons into sauces as we cook dinner
together. I turn to let you taste if the tang of tomato was lost with
too much salt. I go to sleep warm, knowing you will be there
tomorrow and the day after that.

during this tremor hour trembling a time when hotels are full of
people waking to fuck, a three thirty in the morning grey haze and
mouths full of cunts and cocks all around us the soil torn ripped
pocked and stretch marked with the slip of cum you pull out of
yourself above me a slit of bluing sky through a window slatted
with blinds and everything california-whitewashed a sand beach
across the freeway outside and seagulls above earthquake scars
layered with palm fronds you have taken to shedding, tight fisting
your cock while i watch the waves smash you watch a stream roll
down my collar bone the side of my neck a tidal line the ruptures
of hills and white clouds over white-marbled architectures with
lacy-tunneled holes like coral reefs on fault lines over cracked earth
you touch the cum on my shoulder, let me taste it, the air full of
ocean salt mixed with diesel and gas, slate exposed, a tectonic
terrain of valleys lived on by the stars we rarely catch sight of, there
is nothing for me to do but lie back as you touch your mouth to the
upper curve of your own left shoulder, it lets you cum all the easier
all over me we are here where dust bowl states emptied, here in
seismic rushes you decide to no longer even bother with my cunt
i am left sliced open on my back dripping cum flows towards
ground to the san andreas fault line, faulted, my fault but, still,
you will leave me, without a doubt.

acknowledgments

I believe writers are in debt both to other writers and to the people who introduce us to those writers.

This book would not have been possible had a librarian in the Port Clements Public Library on Haida Gwaii not let me check out Judy Blume's *Forever* when I was eight years old. This book would also not have been possible had my mother not given me *Fear of Flying* by Erica Jong when I was eleven years old, followed by *Parachutes & Kisses* when I was fourteen. Thanks, then, to a librarian in a small logging town, and to my mum.

I am also thankful for the books *Bear* and *By Grand Central Station I Sat Down and Wept*. With those two texts, Marian Engel and Elizabeth Smart truly wrote into being new and innovative spaces for Canadian women. I am ever thankful for the courage it must have taken to write such words, to open such spaces.

Finally, there is another writer I am more closely and perhaps more deeply in debt to: without the rigour, patience, humour, political savvy and tremendous attention to detail so generously offered to me by Hiromi Goto, I suspect this book wouldn't be nearly what it is today. Thank you, Hiromi. And to everyone at NeWest — very importantly Lou Morin — who introduced this book to you.

Sarah de Leeuw grew up in Duncan on Vancouver Island, in Port Clements and Queen Charlotte City on Haida Gwaii (The Queen Charlotte Islands), and in Terrace in northern British Columbia. She currently lives in Prince George, B.C., where she is an assistant professor with the Northern Medical Program at the University of Northern British Columbia, the Faculty of Medicine at the University of British Columbia. She has a Ph.D. in cultural-historical geography and has lived and worked in Arizona as a visiting Fulbright scholar with the University of Arizona. She earned a B.F.A. in Creative Writing from the University of Victoria, after which she spent time teaching English in South Korea. She has also worked as a tugboat driver, a women's centre coordinator, a logging camp cook, and a journalist and correspondent for magazines and newspapers in northern B.C. and for CBC Radio's *BC Almanac*. De Leeuw is a two-time recipient a CBC Literary Award in the Creative Nonfiction category, winning first place for "Columbus Burning" in 2008, and second place for "Quick-quick. Slow. Slow." in 2009. Her first book, *Unmarked: Landscapes Along Highway 16*, was published by NeWest Press in 2004.